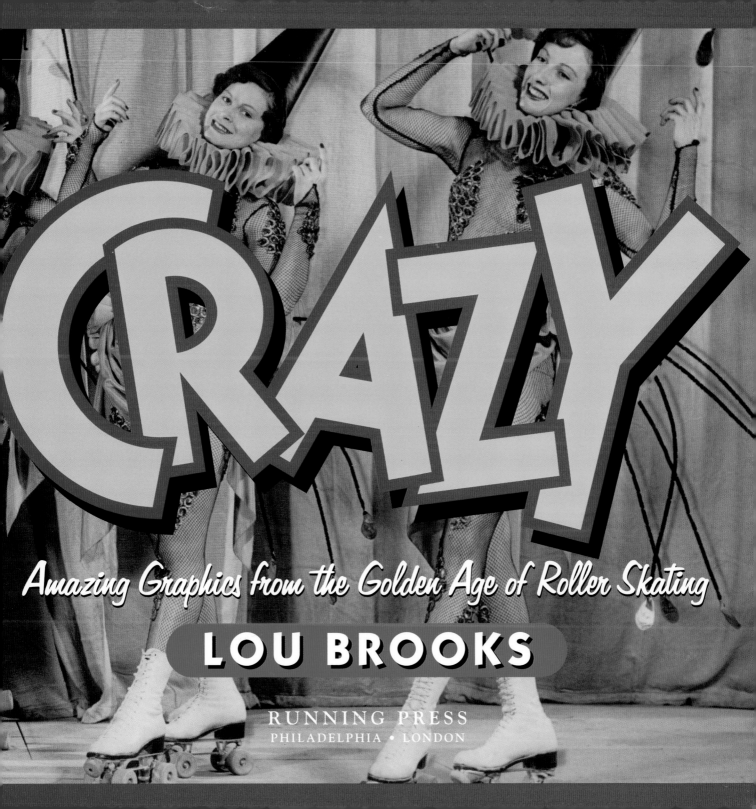

CRAZY

Amazing Graphics from the Golden Age of Roller Skating

LOU BROOKS

Running Press
PHILADELPHIA • LONDON

9 8 7 6 5 4 3 2 1
Digit on the right indicates the number of this printing

Library of Congress Control Number: 2002095660

ISBN 0-7624-1460-X

Written and designed by Lou Brooks
Cover design by Michael Doret
Cover illustration by Lou Brooks
Edited by Joelle Herr
Image restoration by Clare Vanacore
Typography: Neutraface and Kabel

This book may be ordered by mail from the publisher.
Please include $2.50 for postage and handling.
But try your bookstore first!

Running Press Book Publishers
125 South Twenty-second Street
Philadelphia, Pennsylvania 19103

Visit us on the web!
www.runningpress.com

Acknowledgments

Skate Crazy could not have been done without the talent,
support, and generosity of many people. Very special
thanks to: The National Museum of Roller Skating, particularly to Director and Curator Deborah L. Wallis, as well as
Vice President (and unofficial skating historian) Chester
Fried; Susan Curtis, Jim Turner, Sarah Webber, and Scott
A. Wilhite for providing invaluable documentation of the
Golden Age; Joel and David Aranson at Chicago Roller
Skate Co. for permission to use items from their company's
illustrious history; and George Robbins, Nancy Trombetti,
and the amazing C. W. Lowe (see page 10) for giving me
their early-on encouragement.

Also, the most heartfelt gratitude to: Michael Doret, who,
as a designer and friend, has never disappointed me;
Clare Vanacore, who literally put her life on hold in order
to save mine; Buz Teacher, Carlo DeVito, Rachel Cabrera,
Bill Jones, and Kaz at Running Press, all of whom made
this project a pleasure; Jim Heimann, Jill Turney, and
Magician of the Keyboard Dominic Cangelosi for extreme-
ly useful advice and information; and Elwood Smith,
Maggie Pickard, Nancy Stahl, Peter Hoey, Sylvia Chevrier,
Monte Beauchamp, Paul Rogers, Jill Von Hartman, Laura
Smith, Joe Kramer, Debbie Larkin, Ann Middlebrook, Ira
Shapiro, John Baeder, Brad Benedict, Bob Staake, David
Burd, Ron Amistadi, Myra Bach, Mike Bandel, Ray Lammie,
Charles Young, and Fred Slopey for helping me through a
few of life's hair-raising moments.

And finally to my editor, Joelle Herr, who understood from
the start what it means to be "skate crazy," and guided me
through my first major book project with an expert but
gentle hand.

Endpapers: art by Margaret J. Sanders for Carey's Circus
Garden, Philadelphia, Pennsylvania; pages 2-3: The Circus
Harlequins from Skating Vanities of 1951; page 4: postcard detail
from Jolly Time Roller Rink, Fort Worth, Texas; contents page:
sticker detail of skater from Pampa Skating Club, Pampa, Texas.

The National Museum of Roller Skating is located at 4730 South
Street, Lincoln, Nebraska 68506, or visit their web site at
www.rollerskatingmuseum.com.

Skating Program
for This Evening

We are proud to feature our Wurlitzer Grande Pipe Organ for your skating pleasure.

If you wish to practice dances during "All Skate," please restrict your skating to the center of rink.

Dedicated to Clare, who has caused so many miracles to happen—this book being one of them—and who often times has said, "No skating in the house, please!!"

8

Preface

To get off on the right foot with you (awful pun intended), I *haven't* been collecting roller skating stickers all my life, as you'd probably love to believe. Truth is that over a decade ago I was astounded by an immense collection of roller rink memorabilia that I found piled in boxes and scrapbooks at the 26th Street flea market in Manhattan. I convinced my wife and a friend with a car to help me lug it all back to our apartment on 55th Street. I've been lugging it around like a boat anchor ever since, allowing it to take up valuable living space and scratch good hardwood floors—but always determined to transform it into a beautiful book someday, which it now is.

Turning it into that book presented many challenges, not the least of which was having to digitize and then painstakingly repair the damage that cellophane tape had done over the years to each and every sticker. Before the arrival of the computer, the task would have been impossible. In the process, I've tried to walk that delicate line of restoring each item, while not interfering with its original integrity—regardless of how basic the printing and materials often were.

I've defined the "Golden Age" as 1937-1959, even though the vintages of a few images in this book fall slightly outside of those years. They were simply just too good not to be included. Actually, choosing the perfect years to define the Golden Age was difficult. Beginning with 1937 was easier because it was the founding of the Roller Skating Rink Operators Association. Picking an ending turned out to be much more subjective and emotional—more of a feeling, not just about roller rinks, but about the world itself. Certainly many rinks thrived beyond 1959. But what had changed? Us, maybe. I finally decided that the Golden Age ended just after they stopped putting tail fins on cars but before the Beatles arrived. There, that's as close as I can get.

Hey, I hear that mighty Wurlitzer warming up for the "Moonlight Number." So get out there, and if you fall, try your best not to take your date down with you, okay?

— Lou Brooks

A throng of masqueraders from the Children's Safety Skating Club eagerly awaits the start of the annual Arena Gardens Halloween roller skating party in Detroit, 1938.

Shreveport, La. Jan. 27-'27
Mont Robertson defeats Lowe
5 Min 1/2 Mile Race time 1:43

L. A. HIGHWAY OFFICER

ROLLER RINK SKATE CHECK 7481

JACK'S ROLLER RINK 10c
WE RESERVE THE RIGHT
LICENSE GRANTED BY TI...
NATIONAL TICKET CO....

10

Eight Wheels—No Brakes!

Long before roller disco and roller blades, thousands of roller skating rinks were as much a centerpiece of American popular culture as any nightclub or movie theater. By the time the country began to leave the Great Depression behind, roller skating reigned second only to bowling as the most popular participation sport in the country. By 1942, there were more than 3,000 roller skating rinks in America and over ten million Americans skating in them—a long golden era that was to last through the patriotic wartime '40s and into the atomic tail fin decade that followed. Each week, for hundreds of thousands of those people, the local rink became an intimate part of their lives. Often combining the refinement and formality of ballroom dancing and "proper" courtship with the twentieth-century fascination for all things mechanical and moving, the roller rink was a mecca of recreation unlike any other. A high-toned Fred Astaire ballroom on ball bearings, it could also be your very own private amusement park ride beneath your feet. "Eight Wheels, No Brakes!" as some of the ads said.

Facing page: Rink promoter C.W. Lowe challenges motorcycle racer A.H. "Monk" Robertson and his Harley-Davidson to a half-mile match race at Lowe's Shreveport, Louisiana, rink. Robertson won the 1925 race by a distance of only five feet.

The idea of the American roller skating rink, however, was actually born twice—once in the genteel late 1800s and again in 1937. The first incarnation surfaced right in the suppressed mannerly midst of the Victorian Era. By then, the American upper class had reached their own style of sophistication, respected and admired somewhat by the rest of the world, and new things such as the motor car and the roller skate helped nurture their desires to be *moderne*. Roller skating rinks were thereby often found in the best neighborhoods of the most populated cities. Many offered such amenities as professional skating exhibition and instruction, enormous wooden skating floors surrounded by opulent carpeted parlor-like settings, and even ballroom skating to a full thirty-piece brass band.

As rink managers would sadly discover, there was a price to pay for their small role in easing Victorian formality, and it eventually contributed to their own undoing. As the capricious interest of the upper class waned, many rinks degenerated into an atmosphere of honky tonk. Soon, the more poorly managed rinks were going out of business at a dreadful pace. By 1887, very few rinks existed outside of Chicago, and by 1910, there were only an estimated 150 left in the entire country.

TRYING TO GO BOTH WAYS.

Left: In 1885, this novel warning card was handed out to rowdy wrong-way skaters.

Top: The 1926 floor staff from Lowe's Rink, Lincoln, Nebraska, poses for a friendly portrait.

Facing page: The feel of a traveling tent rink was by nature very carnival-like, as demonstrated by this one from 1924.

American roller skate manufacturers were left with a product not many Americans seemed to want anymore, and they despairingly looked for new markets. In 1907, an American skater named Chester Park, sponsored by the Samuel Winslow Roller Skate Company, went to Liverpool, England, and discovered an old building, complete with maple parquet floor. With the Winslow Company's blessing, Park opened an American-style rink that became so successful that he found he had launched a wave of roller rink mania all over England. Soon, roller skating clubs flourished throughout much of Europe. Had roller skating mercifully been given a second chance? Unfortunately, the phenomena was cut short by World War I, and most European rinks, lavish as many were, closed almost as quickly as they had opened. By the time the War was over, roller skating was far from Europe's mind. Wanting to forget the agonies of the Great War, Europeans had caught the exciting new fever of the Jazz Age,

and many rinks that had sat dark and empty for years re-opened, finding new life as dance halls and jazz clubs.

Back in the States, the Victorian Era had given way to the wilder and rougher times that followed—the First World War, the Roaring Twenties, and, finally, the Great Depression. Some struggling rinks gave it a good go to promote sagging business—from staging match races between speed skaters and motorcycles to featuring splashy vaudevillian acts, such as The World-Famous Two Kays, who entered the rink skating on the roof of a moving car, or the all-female Busby Berkeley-like skating revue of Helen Reynolds and Her World Champions. But as hard as rink

Above: The World-Famous Two Kays demonstrate their astonishing skill in 1935.

Facing page: During the '20s and '30s, just about every vaudeville show included a roller skating act. You can almost hear the orchestra belting out "The Sabre Dance."

Helen Reynolds
AND HER
WORLD'S CHAMPIONS ON RICHA

owners tried through it all, they didn't fare much better than their European friends, and most rinks deteriorated into the seedy haunts of society's shadier element. Tough underworld characters, as well as loud and sometimes dangerous adolescent hoodlums, had become common habitués, and bouncers were hired to keep fighting, hazardous horseplay, and chewing tobacco on the skating surface at a minimum. When police failed to turn up the criminal-of-the-moment in bars, bowling alleys, boxing gymnasiums, and pool halls, they would quite often find the culprit at the local rink. Roller skating had strayed far from the gentrified family image it had enjoyed years earlier.

Then, in 1937, seventeen rink owners changed the skating world by meeting at the Arena Gardens roller rink in Detroit during the first national speed skating championships. They had come to Detroit hellbent on straightening out roller skating's lurid reputation, and hopefully saving what was left of the industry. With that in mind, they formed the Roller Skating Rink Operators Association (RSROA), devoted to restoring the image of the rink as a fun, wholesome, safe, clean place for working- and middle-class families. At that meeting, each man anted up a dollar to finance their new dream and declared their headquarters to be a desk drawer in the Gardens main office. The true Golden Age of the Roller Rink was born.

From their meeting in Detroit, the seventeen brought back to each of their own establishments a long new list of rules and ideas that made it clear to the "shadier element" that they were by no means welcome. Dress codes were strictly encouraged—tie and collar for men (no vest unless worn with a jacket!) and knee-length dresses for women (never pants!). Men were also prohibited from wearing sweaters or suspenders, and were also forbidden from wearing uniforms unless they were members of the military. On the other hand, smart uniforms were mandatory for rink employees, making them easily recognizable to any skater needing assistance. Patrons were obliged to follow a well-mannered protocol, such as: "A gentleman should never approach a lady to ask her to skate, unless formally introduced at the request of the lady." Also, rink employees were instructed to always address patrons as either "Miss" or "Mr."

Facing page: Helen Reynolds and Her World's Champions are the "cat's meow" in this 1935 publicity photo. Richardson Skates was the first company to introduce low-maintenance skates to roller rinks.

SKATES.

You might think that such stuffy rules would have made attending a rink too much of a bother in the modern America of the late '30s, especially for young people. Much of rink skating up to that point had evolved through the wild years of the Jazz Age into an American style of jitterbug and jive steps done to a fast tempo—lots of fun, but an uneasy reminder of roller skating's former rough-and-tumble life. In order to make the entire family welcome, the RSROA introduced elegance and etiquette into an evening of skating, while keeping enough of the jive—a step in the right direction that made an evening at the rink appealing to all. It was a balance that enabled the rinks to attract both the wholesome classic skaters and—as long as good manners prevailed—youthful jitterbuggers as well. As time passed, the rules tended to ease up, but during the first few RSROA years, all patrons seemed to be happy with the rink as a sort of rolling royal ballroom for the American middle class.

Though less than ten percent of all rink operators joined the RSROA before 1948, the organization's efforts to clean up roller skating's act were contagious, and the sport prospered with its new image, even among rinks that were not RSROA members. Rinks of all sizes and style began to emerge until there were thousands everywhere, most of them concentrated in the New York, Pennsylvania, and Ohio area—as well as Texas, California, and the upper midwest Great Lakes region. In the South, thanks in part to milder weather, portable roller skating rinks operated by companies such as C. W. Lowe or American Roller Portable Rink were most typically found, traveling from rural town to town like a carnival and setting up for anywhere from a few days to a full three-month season, depending upon the town's population.

Facing page: During the early '30s, hard times demanded clever and ambitious promotion from rink owners to stay in business. In 1931, at the age of 40, speed skater Bill Henning undertook a cross-country trip on roller skates from Carlin's Roller Rink in Baltimore, Maryland, to San Diego, California. Followed by the support car shown here, he covered the distance in 69 days—using up five pairs of skating boots and 127 sets of wheels.

Above: *Despite the benefits brought about by the RSROA, this 1948 sticker shows that not all rinks were eager to become members.*

STARTED CARLIN'S ROLLER RINK ENTERTAINMENT BALTO. Md. DEC. 3? 1931

CHARDS SKATES

MAKE A DATE TO SKATE
CARLIN'S PARK
BALTIMORE'S FRIENDLY ROLLER RINK

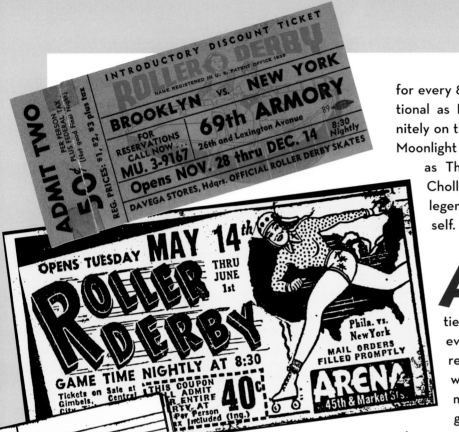

for every 80,000 people. With names as inspirational as Dreamland ("featuring Ray Boughmar nitely on the Mystery Console!"), Crystal Palace, Moonlight Gardens, and Chez Vous, or as artless as The Rip Van Winkle Bowlerskate and Cholly's Rollatorium, many rinks became as legendary and as popular as roller skating itself. America had gone *skate crazy*.

As competition in the major, more-populated markets snowballed, many rinks kept improving amenities and devising clever promotions and events to convince skaters to return as regular customers. Besides offering a well-stocked refreshment bar and the mandatory skate rental counter, owners got carried away with such crowd-pleasers as dazzling neon lighting that changed with the mood of each musical number and "floating" maple floors that put enough spring beneath your skates to make it seem like you were skating on a cloud. Any excuse for endless sorts of weekly and special parties and events became customary in order to guarantee public turnout—from free ordinary weekly skating instructions ("Waltz! Tango! Fox Trot! It's Easy!")

Following the end of World War II, the skating boom really took hold, bigger than any before it. Coaxed on by the immense popularity of a new "sport" on TV called "roller derby," as well as Skating Vanities, roller skating's touring answer to The Ice Capades, rink construction hit an all-time high, reaching several thousand rinks by mid-century—at least one rink

and children's matinees to more flamboyant extravaganzas like Carnival Night, Ladies' Pajama Night (!), and even a Sadie Hawkins' Day Party ("Cash prizes for best costumes from the Li'l Abner comic strip!"). And, of course, no rink was complete without the booming strains of the granddaddy of them all, the "mighty" Wurlitzer organ.

Most rinks also offered skates and accessories for sale rather than for rent at their "skate shoppe," and owning your own roller skates meant you were just one step away from a snazzy metal skate case in which to carry them. Rink owners noticed that the skate cases—available from a variety of manufacturers in just about any color combination or elaborate design you could think of—were often selling as quickly and sometimes even faster than the skates themselves. Besides the practicality, you just had to have one!

Owners had been promoting their rinks all along through the usual techniques of local public relations such as flyers, newspapers, and radio. But thanks to the proliferation of skate cases—most of which came with roomy, ready-made "advertising" space on both sides—a few of the more flamboyant promoters came up with a method unique to the roller rink business, namely *the roller skating sticker*. Given away at the ticket booth, snack stand, skate rental counter, or skate shoppe, stickers were snatched up by loyal skaters who were happy to display them on their skate cases as proud, personalized evidence

STICKERS EXCHANGE
MEET AT
GAY BLADES RINK
NEW YORK
OCT. 1·2·3-48
WELCOME
MARTIN'S SILK SCREEN
GREENVILLE, OHIO

of their loyalty to their home rink. Even if the manufacturer had incorporated its own design onto the case, rink owners noticed that roller skaters preferred to redecorate their case with the free stickers from their home rink.

Other rinks followed suit, and soon there wasn't a roller skating rink anywhere that didn't offer a sticker of its own. Some naively amusing, some confoundingly astonishing, many transcendently beautiful, skating stickers were soon not only being pasted onto skate cases, but were also fervently circulated, collected, and traded by skaters across America. Called "pasters" by collectors, stickers varied in value, depending upon such distinctions as number of colors, unusual die-cuts, and the location of the rink itself. Stickers from overseas, for example, were highly prized and were considered exceptionally collectible.

It wasn't long before sticker collectors decided to make their fun official, and in 1948, twenty-two of them organized the Universal Roller Skating Sticker Exchange (URSSE). That year, they held their first of many annual conventions at the Gay Blades Roller Rink in New York City. From then on, a convention was held each year at a different rink somewhere in the United States, where old and new members alike showed up with scrapbooks and photo albums filled with their pasters. It quickly became sort of a Raccoon

Who Was M.J.S.?

The names of the artists who created the stickers in this book shall forever remain a mystery—they just didn't get to sign their art. Most worked in printing production departments, and the rest were probably friends and relatives of rink owners.

An exception to the rule was Margaret J. Sanders (1900–1981), the woman behind the monogram "M.J.S." which can be found on many of the stickers throughout *Skate Crazy*. Sort of the "Brenda Starr" of skating artists, she was highly independent in the days when women weren't supposed to be, and was very popular as an artist, writer, poet, and competitive skater in her own right.

Beginning in 1928, her art was regularly featured in various ice and roller skating magazines. Operating successfully for decades out of her New Haven, Connecticut, studio, she offered sticker art, greeting cards, wearing apparel, and program cover art that were much adored by roller skaters and ice skaters alike.

Lodge on wheels for sticker-collecting men and women across the country, enabling them to meet, skate, and share their unique peculiar passion with one another. Many became the dearest of friends for life, joyfully trading their precious stickers at the various conventions and events or by mail.

Roller rink skating was an extremely sociable recreation just by its very nature. It seemed local private skating parties were always being organized by one group or another, and many skaters kept in touch year-round with such things as homemade greeting cards and party announcements. But members of the URSSE seemed to bring even more to it, criss-crossing the country every year, often coast to coast and always at their own expense, just to be together and allow their prized sticker collections to mingle and be admired by other members. The roller rink sticker had become an officially collectible *objet d' art*—sort of like stamp collecting, only you got to have fun!

Between 1948 and 1980, URSSE membership grew to over 4,000 collectors from 48 states and five foreign countries. Rink promoters became so aware of collectors and the impact the stickers had upon the public that thousands of stickers were produced well into the 1970s.

The last annual convention was attended by what was left of a sparse URSSE membership on July 29, 1989, at a rink in Cornwells Heights, Pennsylvania. The glitter days of roller disco had come and gone. The soft neon pink and blue glow of artificial moonlight and well-mannered socializing to the mighty Wurlitzer were not so needed in a world where they roller blade in the street and skateboard on the sidewalk. Realizing their beloved Raccoon Lodge really belonged in a different time and place, members voted at that convention to disband. What they left behind for us are thousands of "pasters"—each an amazing reflection of the Golden Age of skating rinks, and a reflection of ourselves as well.

UNIVERSAL · ROLLER · SKATING · STICKER · EXCHANGE
MEMBER U·R·S·S·E
ALL OVER THE WORLD

A Very Short History of Roller Skates

Believe it or not, roller skates have been with us in some form or another since at least around 1760, although it wasn't exactly a happy beginning. That's when the first documented pair was invented in London by Joseph Merlin, a then well-known musical instrument maker, clock maker, and robot builder. Merlin was delighted with his ingenious new form of mobility and keen on demonstrating it to his high society friends. One evening, while attending a fancy masquerade party at Carlisle-House on Soho Square, he found the tiny wheels of his contraption impossible to control and quickly wore out his welcome by skating into a large expensive mirror at high speed. He destroyed the mirror, his violin, and nearly himself.

Thanks in part to Merlin literally crashing the party and the embarrassing publicity that followed, roller skating wasn't exactly embraced by English society, and not much more was heard of it for several decades. But as the world moved toward and into the nineteenth century, various forms of the roller skate emerged once again, often to accommodate theatrical productions involving the illusion of "ice skating," on a typically wooden stage.

In 1849, around the time French inventor Louis Legrand invented a type of roller skate that was fairly maneuverable, the extremely popular German composer Giacomo Meyerbeer was putting together the opera, "Le Profete." Meyerbeer was widely known for his elaborate crowd-pleasing productions.

Having seen a demonstration of Legrand's skates, he added an entire spectacular winter ice carnival scene to the work and hired Legrand to make roller skates for the entire *corps de ballet* and teach them how to use them. The premiere in Berlin was such a success that a major tour followed, including a well-received engagement in Paris. By the 1850s, skating was all the rage in many European cites.

But it wasn't until 1863 that the modern roller skate—two wheels in back, two in front—was invented in the United States by James Plimpton. Most importantly, his patent included an oscillating action that allowed the skater to lean into a turn. At last a roller skater could glide along as gracefully as any ice skater. Three years later, as public enthusiasm for roller skating grew, Plimpton realized he needed to promote his idea and sell skates. He converted the dining room of Atlantic House, a fashionable resort in Newport, Rhode Island, into a skating area for guests—introducing America to its first roller rink.

By the 1880s, roller rinks had popped up in New York, Boston, Chicago, and many other cities. American industry found itself cranking out Plimpton-style skates by the thousands. Although many companies offered several models to choose from, each basic skate featured the same oscillating action with wood, metal, or ivory wheels, and was strapped onto the shoe front and back. Sound familiar? The roller skate was ensconced in American culture for good!

Formally trained in ballet, Gloria Nord was to roller skating what Sonja Henie was to ice skating. She was best known as the star attraction of "Skating Vanities," a spectacular show on roller skates that toured America and Europe from 1942 to 1956. Here, her beauty graces the cover of the Vanities program from 1946.

Isn't She Lovely?

When Irving Berlin wrote "A Pretty Girl is Like a Melody" for the Ziegfeld Follies back in 1919, he seemed to inspire the promotional approach that many roller skating rink owners would take years later. Pairing the image of a pretty girl with the task of selling skating tickets proved to be very successful during the Golden Age. Short skirt, beautiful legs, high-laced skates, her figure frozen in a graceful pose as she seemed to spin and fly so effortlessly through the air—now *that's* advertising! Ironically, many rinks enforced a very puritanical dress code, particularly in reference to women. Acceptable attire for women meant a knee-length dress or skirt, and never slacks.

Left: Roller Skating Almanac enticed readers with its "Mystery Girl." *Right:* This lovely lady was the main attraction on a sticker from The Market Roller Rink in Oklahoma City.

In the days of the Second World War, just about every soldier had a picture of a pin up girl in his foot locker. Nothing bolstered the image of a lovely skating lass more than Skating Vanities, with its endless parade of beautiful women on roller skates.

The 1942 brainchild of former boxing promoter Harold Steinman, it was roller skating's answer to The Ice Follies and toured America and Europe successfully until 1956. Much of it was designed around its star, Gloria Nord, a beautiful, talented skater discovered by Mickey Rooney at the opening of the Roller Bowl in Hollywood.

In 1944, movie producers at 20th Century Fox decided that Skating Vanities was the perfect backdrop

ALL YEAR ROUND

SKATELAND

WILLOW GROVE PARK

ROLLER SKATING NIGHTLY

STATE SKATING RINK

HAMMOND IND.

EDGEWATER ROLLER RINK

EDGEWATER PARK · CELINA-O

ORCHARD ISLAND SKATING RINK

INDIAN LAKE - OHIO

LAKE LENAPE R K

MAYS LANDING, N.J.

...ME AT HOLCOMB'S ROLLER RINK

4 TH. PLAIN AND STAPELTON ROAD

VANCOUVER WASHINGTON

HOLCOMB'S RECREATION HALL

Holland's SKATELAND

1035 STATE STREET

BRIDGEPORT, CONN

BARBER'S SKATELAND

GEORGIAVILLE

RHODE ISLAND

ROLL-O-RINK

THE RINK OF REFINEMENT

HAMMOND ORGAN

PITTSBURGH

IN SHERADEN ONE SQUARE FROM LANGLEY HI PHONE FED.-3434

Meet Me at Skateland

1990 South Broadway Denver, Colo.

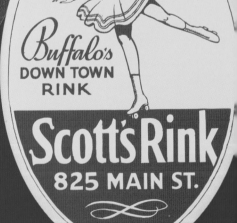

Buffalo's DOWN TOWN RINK

Scott's Rink

825 MAIN ST.

REDONDO
BEACH ROLLER RINK

WASHINGTON'S
LARGEST · AND · FINEST

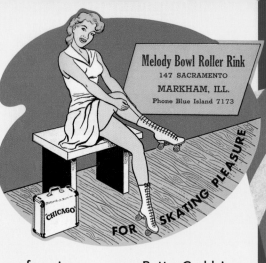

for pin up queen Betty Grable's next picture. And the title? "Pin Up Girl," of course. Gloria was included in the cast, but her love of the skating rink prevailed over pursuit of any motion picture career. Life in Hollywood was left to Sonja Henie, her ice skating counterpart.

By the early '50s, Gloria left the Vanities to star in an ice skating show in England as Sleeping Beauty. She was replaced as star of the Vanities by world roller skating figure champion Peggy Wallace.

ERN PARKWAY
ROLLER SKATING RINK

435 EASTERN PARKWAY (nr. HOWARD AVE.) BROOKL

Left: Skating Vanities star Gloria Nord's balletic background shines through in this spectacular leap to publicize the 1948 show. *Far right:* The tall Texas skater in the green dress is part of a sticker from Cook's Roller Rink, advertised as "Houston's Largest."

SEPIA SKATING CLUB

PHILADELPHIA'S LARGEST

MOST MODERN RINK

SKATING
EVERY TUESDAY EVENING

71ST & GRAYS AVE.

Hail to the Queen...

What could be more exciting than a beauty pageant?... a beauty pageant on roller skates! In its January 1940 issue, *Nation's Skater Magazine* proclaimed the very first national roller skating queen contest. Soon rinks around the country were adding a touch of "glamour" to their image by each crowning their own special queen, with royal titles ranging from Miss Mammoth Gardens to Queen of the Skating Mermaids.

In 1950, the RSROA stepped in with an annual Roller Skating Queen of America contest in association with their National Roller Skating Championships—a tradition that was to last 26 years. There were contestants from every state, and the reigning Queen got to hand out the medals to the Championship winners. While the ladies were not judged on their skating abilities, the earliest rules stated that "each contestant will be judged on beauty alone but must be able to skate."

Miss Nebraska, Miss Colorado, and Miss Missouri greet their loyal subjects from their parade float during the 1962 RSROA National Championships in Lincoln, Nebraska.

QUEENS & HORACE HARDING BOULEVARDS

Queens

ROLLER RINK

...MHURST, LONG ISLAND, N.Y.

ORANGEBURG PLAYLAND INC.

ROLLER RINK

RT. 303 & 340

ORANGEBURG, N.Y.

ROLLER RINK

PALACE ROLLER RINK

ON
NORTH SCHUYLER
AVENUE

KANKAKEE
ILLINOIS

TECH ROLLERWAY

84 MASS. AVE.
CAMBRIDGE, MASS.

Cros

24th ♦ LEAVENWORTH

ROL
The

Peggy Wallace and her partner Frank Foster offer a supreme example of focused artistry during their "Bolero" number for a 1950s tour of Skating Vanities. The show offered over 40 specialty and production numbers, as well as Ole Olsen & Chic Johnson as the show's madcap comedic hosts.

Let's Dance!

THE ONLY KNEE ACTION
SKATING FLOOR IN
THE COUNTRY

SWANK Rink

WESTERN AVE. at 111th STREET
CHICAGO, ILL.

ROLLER SKATE AND KEEP FIT!

LOON LAKE PAVILION

R.F.D NO. 1
IRONS, MICHIGAN

Whenever it came to dancing at the rink, most skaters in the '50s and '60s never got much fancier than the good old Hokey Pokey. Originally recorded in the late '40s by Larry LaPrise and the Ram Trio for the Sun Valley, Idaho, ski crowd, the Hokey Pokey was possibly the most embarrassing dance ever created—even if you *weren't* on roller skates. It basically involved all skaters lining the rink in a huge circle and, as the song lyrics named various body parts, skaters would try to do their best to "shake it all about" on cue. With a few hun-

Palace

ROLLER RINK
WHERE SKATING IS A PLEASURE

HAMMOND, IND.

wn

OMAHA, NEBRASKA

RINK
ance Rink"

STONE STREET
ARENA
Waltzing
CLUB

ALBERT LEA MINN.

NEW ULM MINN.

CARL'S ROLLER RINKS

dred people on skates, it sounded a lot like an elephant stampede. Not the sort of dancing that would require a tuxedo.

Fortunately, for rink patrons who were into something a bit more Astaire-ish, skating served up quite a menu of dancing. In the late '30s, sensing that perhaps a new era was about to begin, Wall Street millionaire and roller skating enthusiast Perry Rawson returned from Europe, determined to infuse the *je ne sais quoi* of European ice dancing into American roller skating. Soon, American rinks were employing skating instructors to demon-

Below: The dreaded "Scram" and "Skidoo" card! Just like at any party, the hosts liked to keep things at the rink moving with interesting games, often turning the rink into somewhat of a social laboratory. Floor ushers, acting out their version of traffic cop, would slip these cards to unsuspecting couples, urging them to skate the second half of the dance with someone they had never met.

Right: Couples look for fun and romance late '30s-style as they dance their cares away at Dreamland Park, Newark, New Jersey.

BROAD & SPRUCE

PHILA.

DANCE BOX

ROLLER RINK

SKATING EVERY EVENING

Where there's fun there are young people, and skating rinks did their best to get their attention. Pictured above are two panels from "Skating Skills—Secrets of Roller Skating," a promotional comic book for teenagers published in 1957 by the Chicago Roller Skate Co.

Skate!
...FOR EXCITEMENT!
...FOR FUN!

ON "CHICAGO" SKATES

...MAN'S ROLLER RINK
...ORTH TEXAS   FAIRFIELD, CALIFORN...

SCOTTY'S
...OLLER BOWL
...NO, MICHIGAN

FOR Health's Sake
ROLLER SKATE

WORLD FAMOUS
SKATE YOUR DATE
HOLLYWOOD
ROLLERBOWL

PARKVIEW
Roller Rink
AURORA, ILL.
FEATURING...
...THE SENSATIONAL FLOATING FLOOR

THE BLUES NO. 6 (CHOCTAW)

45

OLD DOMINION S SKATING RINK S NEWP

PURPLE PENNANT LAKE STEVENS, WASHINGTON

ROLLER SKATING
Family-Picnics
Group-Picnics
Swimming
Boating
Cabins
Fishing
Open the Year Around

ROLLER SKATING
FOR Youthful SPIRITS

RAINBOW ROLLER DROME
ROLLER SKATING
EVERY NIGHT
WOODSIDE ·PARK· PHILADELPHIA

46

CASHMAN'S ROLLER RINK PORTSMOUTH, R.I.

FLAMINGO • ROLLER PALACE • Pittsburgh

Jam ROLLER SKATING at GAY BLADES 52 ST. & BWAY. N.Y.C. AMERICA'S MOST MAGNIFICENT ROLLER SKATING RINK

Rollerland RSROA •••• RENTON 631 Rainier Ave. AL.5·5417

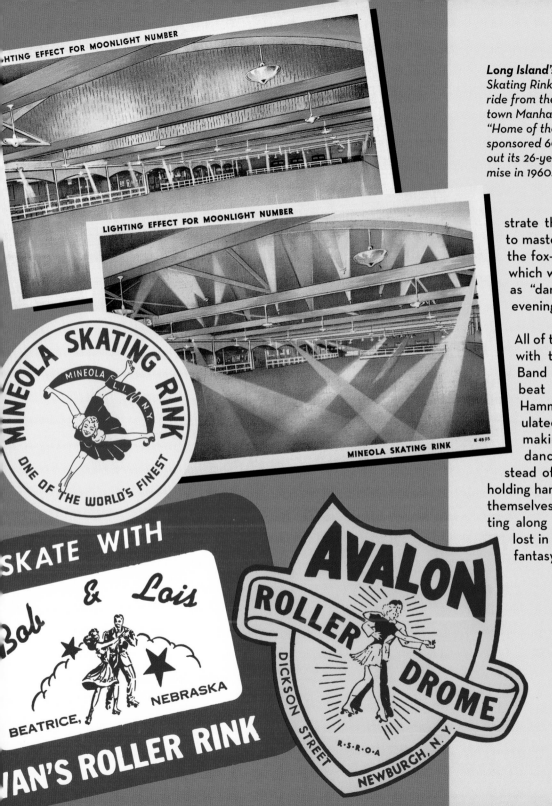

LIGHTING EFFECT FOR MOONLIGHT NUMBER

LIGHTING EFFECT FOR MOONLIGHT NUMBER

MINEOLA SKATING RINK

MINEOLA SKATING RINK

MINEOLA
L.I., N.Y.

ONE OF THE WORLD'S FINEST

SKATE WITH

Bob & Lois

BEATRICE, NEBRASKA

...AN'S ROLLER RINK

AVALON ROLLER DROME

DICKSON STREET

NEWBURGH, N.Y.

R·S·R·O·A

Long Island's beautiful Mineola Skating Rink was but a short train ride from the sophistication of midtown Manhattan. Promoted as "Home of the Dance Skaters," it sponsored 60 skating clubs throughout its 26-year history, until its demise in 1960.

strate the new steps required to master the waltz, the tango, the fox-trot, and the two-step, which were then incorporated as "dance specials" into the evening program.

All of this coincided perfectly with the advent of the Big Band Era. The solid musical beat of the Wurlitzer and Hammond organs easily emulated the Big Band sound, making the elegant new dances very popular. Instead of just skating in circles holding hands, patrons now found themselves waltzing and fox-trotting along under the mirror ball, lost in the dreamy Hollywood fantasy of the nightclub life.

SKATELAND ROLLER RINK
TIFFIN, OHIO

R. S. R. O. A.
MELODEE D & F CLUB
MELODEE ROLLER RINK
SANFORD, FLA.

FAIR PARK
TEXAS
AUTOMOBILE BUILDING
SKATING RINK
SOUTHWEST'S LARGEST AND FINEST
for Health's Sake
ROLLER SKATE
FREE INSTRUCTIONS
ORGAN MUSIC
25¢ - 35¢
SKATES FREE
Listen in WRR -- 10:45 'til 11 P.M.
RACES EVERY SUN. NIGHT
DAILY 7:30 TO 10 P.M.
SAT.-SUN. MATINEE 2:30 TO 5:00
...TIES BY APPOINTMENT

Calling All Skaters - - -
GALA ROLLER ROUND-UP
Greyhounds Skating Club
at the
WHITE HORSE ROLLER RINK
Watsontown, N.J.
SUN. NOVEMBER 10,
Featuring Club Jacket Parade
WALTZ CONTEST
SWING CONTEST
TWO-STEP CONTEST
- Strictly Amateur -
Rink Open 6 p.m. to ?
Spectators: Admission 25c
Phone: 4798-W Novelty PRINTING Service, 734 Federal St., Camden, N. J.

ROLLERDROME
THIRD AND BELL
SEATTLE, WASH.
HAMMOND ORGAN
CHICAGO SKATES
HEALTH · FUN · EXERCISE
ROLLER SKATING

Skate For Health

D & C ROLLER RINK

122-24 E. 3rd St.   Little Rock, Arkansas

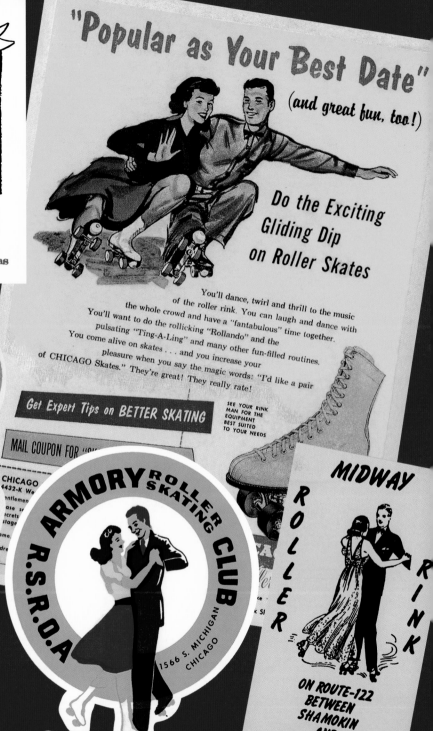

"Popular as Your Best Date"

(and great fun, too!)

Do the Exciting Gliding Dip on Roller Skates

You'll dance, twirl and thrill to the music of the roller rink. You can laugh and dance with the whole crowd and have a "fantabulous" time together. You'll want to do the rollicking "Rollando" and the pulsating "Ting-A-Ling" and many other fun-filled routines. You come alive on skates . . . and you increase your pleasure when you say the magic words: "I'd like a pair of CHICAGO Skates." They're great! They really rate!

Get Expert Tips on BETTER SKATING

SEE YOUR RINK MAN FOR THE EQUIPMENT BEST SUITED TO YOUR NEEDS

MAIL COUPON FOR "SK...

CHICAGO
4432-K We...
...entlemen...
...ase s...
...secrets...
...stage...

...ame...
...ddress...
City...

FOREST PARK ROLLER RINK

GENOA, OHIO
on Routes 20 and 120

Upper right: *A 1959 advertisement for Chicago roller skates explains how doing "the exciting gliding dip" promises a "fantabulous" time together.*

ARMORY ROLLER SKATING CLUB

R.S.R.O.A.

1566 S. MICHIGAN
CHICAGO

MIDWAY ROLLER RINK

ON ROUTE-122
BETWEEN
SHAMOKIN
AND
MT. CARMEL PA.

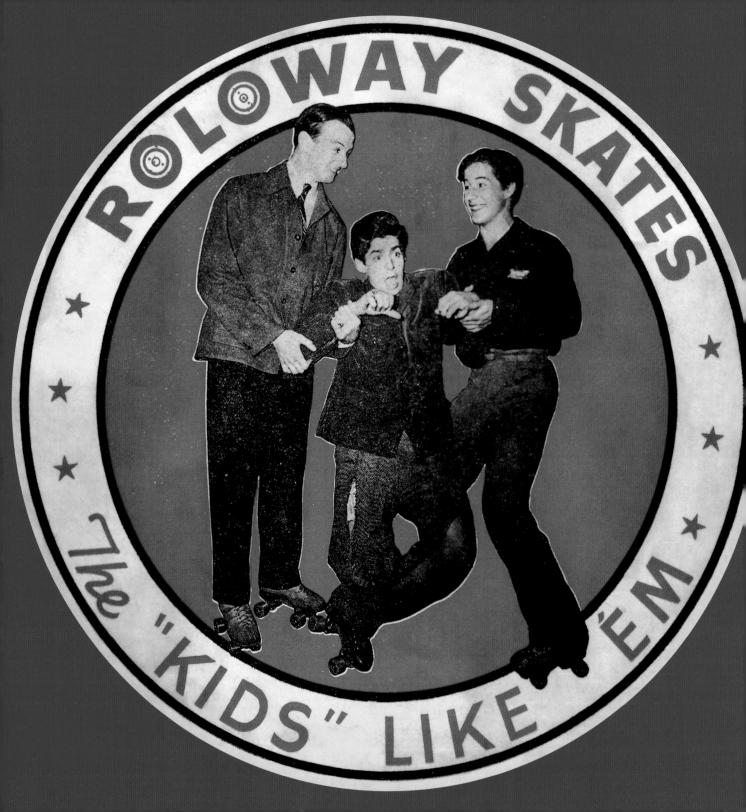

Look Out!

Sometime during the 1920s, C.M. Lowe decided to bring one of his traveling tent rinks to Pittsburg, Kansas. A local newspaper reporter tried it out and wrote, "...the important thing to remember is to circle the center poles without running into mishap or over a fallen skater or...without knocking your own rollers from underneath you."

People have been falling down at skating rinks for a long time, usually injuring little more than their self-image in the "end." It all revolves around the "falling-on-the-banana-peel" principle: if it's happening to someone aside from yourself, it can be very funny.

Hoffman's SKATELAND
ALBANY, N.Y.
1335 CENTRAL AVE.

Yakima Roller Rink
"Best equipped of the Northwests smaller rinks."
409 East Yakima Ave.
SALLY and JAY LaVERGNE Proprietors
Phone 3725
Forced Landing

Atlanta, Ga.

FLORHAM PARK N.J.
Roller Skating ARENA
WHERE YOU ACQUIRE GRACE AND POISE

SKATEMOR RINK
7130 East 14th St.
Oakland, California

IDLE HOUR PARK
ROLLER RINK
South's Largest & Finest Amusement Center
Ala.

CARMAN Skating Rink
GERMANTOWN AV. & ALLEGHENY
PHILA., PA.

55

ROLLERDROME
Atlanta Georgia

SKATE for HEALTH and for VICTORY

Keep 'em Rolling

The end of the Great Depression seemed to be at hand by the late '30s. America found itself finally taking a breather from all of the misery that had been a part of it. There was optimism underfoot, but with it came the certain dread of a World War that lurked upon the horizon.

The bombing of Pearl Harbor at the end of 1941 put an end to any doubts of our involvement. Within a year, hundreds of thousands of young American

GOD BLESS AMERICA

ADELPHIA SPORTING CLUB
39th & MARKET STS.
PHILADELPHIA
SKATING NIGHTLY

WAR BONDS

in America out

your

Compliments of
SO ROBLES ROLLER·RINK
and Park Streets — P. O. Box 703
Paso Robles, California

BUY A BOND AND GET THAT
SKATING BLOND
AND KEEP 'EM ROLLING
DEEP IN THE HEART OF TEXAS
LONE STAR ROLLER RINK
BARSTOW, TEXAS

MEDFORD ROLLER RINK

IMPERIAL RINK
ROLLER *Skating*

SUNDAY
Afternoon
&
Evening

Skating
Days
WED.
FRI.
SAT.

MANKATO

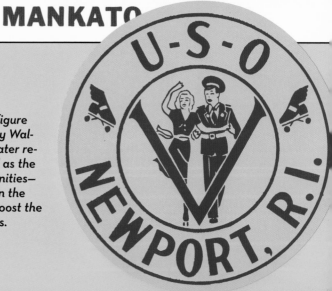

World champion figure roller skater Peggy Wallace—who would later replace Gloria Nord as the star of Skating Vanities—poses backstage in the late '40s to help boost the morale of our boys.

ROLLERDROME

SAINT JOHN NEW BRUNSWICK CANADA

men enlisted to fight in the War—and life as the nation knew it was drastically changed.

Nighttime blackouts to thwart enemy attack brought an end to much of our routine activity. Events such as nighttime baseball and football disappeared. Family motoring, along with the sport of auto racing, was put on hold, due to shortages of parts, gasoline, and rubber. A lack of manpower caused most spectator sports to dwindle to near nonexistence. Even America's latest sport on wheels—the roller derby—dwindled down to one team.

At the same time, roller rinks—along with bowling alleys and movie theaters—thrived. Even amid the hardship of skate parts shortages, rinks provided a warm and friendly place where many

FOR THE DURATION

ROLLERLAND
E. MOUND AT 18th · COLUMBUS, OHIO

PLEDGES TO BUILD: MORALE STAMINA PHYSICAL FITNESS

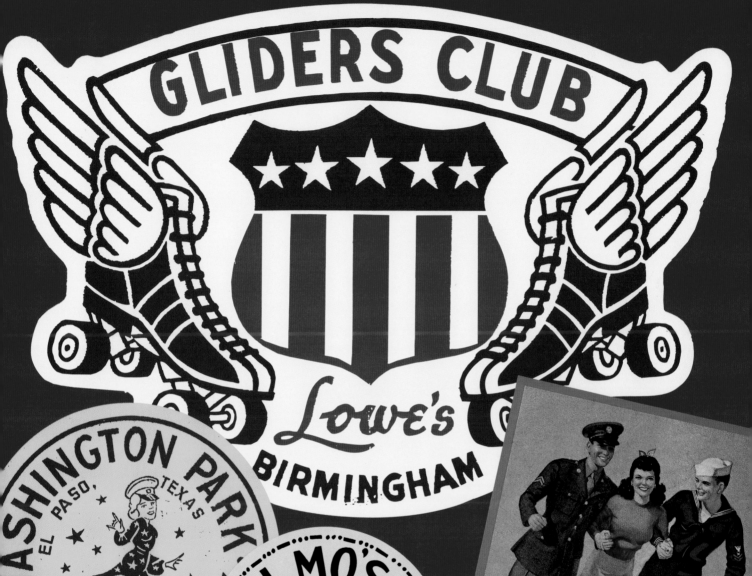

GLIDERS CLUB

Lowe's
BIRMINGHAM

WASHINGTON PARK · ROLLER RINK
EL PASO, TEXAS

ELMO'S ROLLER RINK
BELOIT, WIS.
V FOR VICTORY

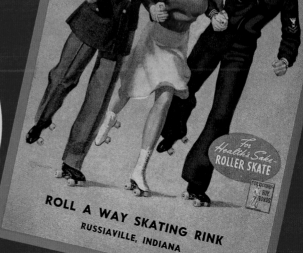

For Health's Sake—
ROLLER SKATE

FOR VICTORY BUY BONDS

ROLL A WAY SKATING RINK
RUSSIAVILLE, INDIANA

war-troubled skaters could forget their problems for a few hours. By regularly hosting scrap, bond, and stamp drives every week, rinks were also successful at supporting the ongoing war effort.

During the War, the ingenious notion of the roller skate had also worked itself into the enterprising minds of the military. In 1942, *Popular Science* reported that the Army was busy developing lightweight skates to be used by the infantry during the gasoline and rubber shortages "as a sure means of getting past bombed streets swiftly and safely."

"Arena Gardens Roller Skating Club"

"KEEP 'EM ROLLING"

V

BROOKLYN
ROLLER SKATING
RINK
BLVD. & NOSTRAND AVE. BKLYN. N.Y.

WE SELL DEFENSE STAMPS TOO. WANT ONE?

YOUR GOVERNMENT
ASKS THAT YOU KEEP FIT

SKATE AT ENJOIE PARK
ENDICOTT JOHNSON
ENDICOTT N.Y.

They Need Scrap.....
LETS SEND IT TO THEM
"VIA" BOMBER
DROP
IRON - BRASS - TINFOIL
RUBBER *IN BARREL*
No Rubber Checks.

The scrap drive during World War II was the granddaddy of modern-day recycling. Arena Gardens manager Fred Martin fishes out a seemingly endless string of keys donated by a generous skater. Note the comment on the sign about checks.

CASINO
VALLEJO
CAL.
FOR VICTORY
"ROLLER RINK"
"HARRY AND GRACE WELCOME YOU"

PALACE SKATING RINK
SULPHUR SPRINGS FLA.
ROLL ON-TO VICTORY

R·A·I·N·B·O·W
WOODSIDE PARK
ROLLER SKATING
EVERY AFTERNOON AND EVENING
ADELPHIA S.C.
ROLLERDROME

KEEP'EM FLYING
RIVER GARDEN
ROLLERDROME
HEALDSBURG, CALIFORNIA
KEEP EM ROLLING

ROLLERDROME
24 E. NOTTINGHAM RD.
DAYTON, OHIO

DOYLE'S SKATING RINK

NEW BRITAIN, CONN.   AN R. S. R. O. A. RINK

LEO DOYLE, Proprietor

No. 835, Copyright 1942, F. P. H. Co., New London, Ohio

WONDER ROLLERS
Sothern Skating Rink
Hatboro, Pa.

ART'S
KEEP 'EM FLYING
PILOTS ON WHEELS
Buy DEFENSE REMEMBER PEARL
BONDS HARBOR

ART'S
SKATELAND
PILOTS ON WHEELS
CONSHOHOCKEN, PA.

ART'S
SKATELAND
PILOTS ON WHEELS
RIDGE PIKE
CONSHOHOCKEN
PA.

All Skate!

Most rinks featured a well-orchestrated evening's "program" of various dances, also referred to as "skates." At the more elaborate rinks, such as New York's Hillside and Gay Blades, Detroit's Arena Gardens, or Sunset Park in Pennsylvania, the program was handsomely printed and handed to each skater as a sou-

Facing page: Happy skaters mingle at the magnificent Idora Roller Skating Palace at Idora Park, Youngstown, Ohio.

HUBERT'S ROLLER RINK

107 East Broadway
PASADENA, TEXAS

ITALIAN VILLAGE
Skating and Dancing
Dallas City, Illinois

HILLSIDE

SKATE YOUR TROUBLES AWAY
AT THE FRIENDLY RINK FOR
FRIENDLY SKATERS

HILLSIDE ROLLER SKATING RINK
HILLSIDE & METROPOLITAN AVE.
RICHMOND HILL 18, N.Y.

RINK

It's **FUN** to Roller Skate!

ALASKAN   752 SOUTH HYDRAULIC
WICHITA 16, KANSAS

venir. Other smaller rinks saved the cost of printing a program by just politely announcing each skate over the address system. Programs usually included every sort of skating dance imaginable, from the simple two-steps, fox trots, and waltzes to intimidating tangos, polkas, and even dances for trios and foursomes.

At the same time, owners wanted their rink to be fun for the entire family—not just dancing couples. They were careful to generously insert into the evening's program the "All Skate," which would allow all skaters out onto the floor.

The All Skate was often completely free form, allowing everyone to enjoy themselves by skating the best they could in time to the music—either alone or as a couple. All kinds of surprises could be thrown in, such as changing directions, following a figure-eight pattern, or having to sing along while you skated. Some rinks had their own version of musical chairs. When the music stopped, skaters scrambled to stand on a special mark on the rink floor, or faced sitting out the rest of the number.

Roller Skating

A BARREL O' FUN

"CHICAGO"

SOUTH AMBOY ARENA
Stevens Avenue and 6th Street
South Amboy, New Jersey

Washington Park
ROLLER RINK

EL PASO,
TEXAS

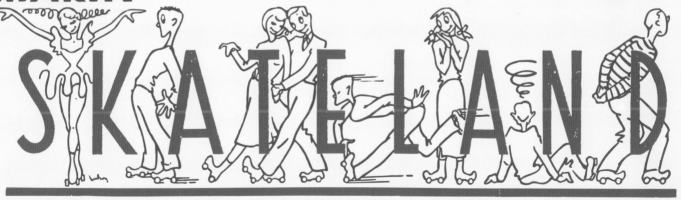

MARIN

RSROA MEMBER

SKATELAND

836 FOURTH ST., SAN RAFAEL, PHONE 6435-W

INSIDE FLOOR CONSISTING OF 12,000 sq.ft. FOR BEGINNERS and FANCY SKATERS.

JOHNSON SKATELA...

10 ST. 6...
EM 4...
DOUGLAS...
Skate to...

Right: In 1938, skaters wait to circle Detroit's Arena Gardens rink floor in rows of eight for the Grand March, a ritual that began every evening's festivities.

Left: Skaters fuel up at the Arena Gardens refreshment counter—in the days of dress codes and bow ties.

Riverside Ballro...
GREEN BAY, WISCONSIN

ROLLER RIN...

ARENA GARDENS
Roller Skating Club
DETROIT

Musical Program

RUSSELL BICE
Organist . . . Wurlitzer Grande Pipe Organ

Let's Dance

1. GREETINGS
2. ALL SKATE .... March
3. ALL SKATE .... Waltz
4. ALL SKATE .... Two-Step
5. COUPLES .... Waltz
   ALL SKATE .... Schottische
   ALL SKATE .... Swing
Let's Dance
COUPLES WALTZ ... { Spread Eagle A / Flirtation / Mohawk / Spread Eagle B }
   SKATE
   SKATE .... Swing
   SWING and SING .... Two-Step
   TE .... Waltz
   Skaters Parade
ERMISSION

REVERSE SKATIN
Rest and Refreshments
Let's Dance
13. COUPLES .... {
14. ALL SKATE
15. LADIES
16. ALL SKATE .... Two
17. ALL SKATE V
Let's Dance
18. COUPLES .... Sw
19. ALL SKATE .... { CALLED DAI
20. ALL SKATE .... Schottisc
Let's Dance
21. COUPLES .... Swing
22. ALL SKATE .... { Fourteen-Step / Continental Waltz / Blues / Keste Fox-Trot }
23. ALL SKATE .... Two-Step
COUPLES
24. Good-Night Dance .... Waltz
   Skates Off .... { WALTZERS ONLY }

Music to Skate By

The introduction of talking motion pictures in 1927 changed everything in Hollywood, and it also had a profound impact on the roller skating industry. To accommodate the "talkies," movie theaters found themselves replacing elaborate multiple-console pipe organs with relatively simpler audio systems.

Theater organists suddenly found themselves scurrying for work, and many ended up performing at the local roller rink. From the 1920s through the 1940s, organ music was considered

LET'S Go Skating AT

TED'S ROLLER RINK HUTCHINSON, MINN.

Skating WED. SAT. SUN.

BLU-C ROLLER RINK

ASTORIA · OREGON AIRPORT ROAD

RAMONA GARDENS Roller Rink Grand Rapids, Michi

SKATING PALACE
FAIRWAY
SANDWICH -ILL.

THE SINGING WHEELS ARENA

UPPER BROAD STREET — — RED BANK, N. J.

Rollercade
SKATING RINK

very contemporary entertainment. Its popularity on the radio led to it being the centerpiece of many homes.

During the '30s—as high society grew tired of the novelty of roller skating and rinks found themselves no longer able to afford the full brass band their upper-class clientele had enjoyed—the organ easily became a mainstay of the roller rink. The more affluent rinks were able to install and maintain the Wurlitzer Organ—granddaddy of the old movie theaters—but most others eventually settled upon the Hammond Electronic Organ, which took up little space and offered a sound and rhythm that adapted very well to the popular roller skating dances.

ELTORIAN
Roller
SKATING RINK

SPECIAL
RATES to
SCHOOLS
CLUBS
ORGANIZATIONS

NOISELESS
CUSHION FLOOR

Call **PEN**ypakr
9746
755 S. 11th ST.

TOM GRIERSON RINK
CHARLOTTE, N.Y.

Organist Russell Bice smiles from high atop his organ loft at Detroit's Arena Gardens. A series of mirrors above his sheet music allowed him to follow the skaters as he played. A favorite among skaters, he remained with the rink during its entire existence from 1935 to 1953.

The sticker to the left was used to promote the song, "I Love to Roller Skate," written and recorded by skating enthusiast Art Grubb in 1943. On the back page of the sheet music, he explained he did it "...for the one thing I owe all the real fun I got out of life to, and that is the beloved sport of roller skating."

The Wild West

Thanks to television, movies, and bronco-bustin' heroes such as Gene Autry and Hopalong Cassidy, American culture experienced a long love affair with the Wild West. Many skating rinks also found themselves under its spell. Interestingly, the term "West of the Pecos" did not always apply—some rinks weren't any farther west than Massachusetts. The photo on the next two pages, for example, was taken on the prairies of Vineland, New Jersey.

PASTIME PARK ROLLER RINK
TUCSON, ARIZONA

SALINAS ROLLERLAND
SALINAS, CALIF.

ATELAND
1006 N. LINCOLN
CASPER WYO.

EAST END ROLLER RINK
ALBUQUERQUE • NEW MEXICO

LAKE CHARGOGGAGOGGMANCHAUGGAGOGGCHAUBUNAGUNGAMAUGG
INDIAN ROLLERS
WEBSTER, MASS.

ROLLER TOMAHAWK RINK
CHEROKEE IOWA

YIP-PEEEEEE! C'MON GANG LET'S GO!
Sleepy Hollow Rink
Rt. 663 - Between Pennsburg & Quakertown Pa

1006 W. Northwest Highway, Arlington Heights, Ill.
Arlington ROLLER RINK

Rollerink

29 PALMS
CALIFORNIA

Rollerdrome

PIKE'S PEAK to the CORN BELT

in Colorado
COLORADO SPRINGS
Pikes Peak Skateland
MANITOU SPRINGS
Manitou Roller Rink
in Iowa
CEDAR FALLS
Black Hawk Roller Rink
AMES
Skateland
20th Century Bowling

Young "cowboys" saddle up their cardboard ponies and roller skates for the "Cowboys of the Wild West" number during the Vineland Roll-O-Capers of 1968.

One of the most interesting speed skaters of all time was Fred "Bright Star" Muree, a Native American who hit his stride during skating's first boom period of the 1880s. Fear of life on an Oklahoma reservation forced him and his family to walk (!) to Boston, where he worked as a "skate boy" for the Plimpton Skate Rink.

He was given a pair of speed skates and entered a five-mile race against seventeen other competitors—including Kenneth Skinner, Boston's fastest skater at the time. Muree won, smashing Skinner's record by eight seconds. When the story hit the newspapers, Muree was hired to race for Boston's Argyle Rink, and from 1880 to 1881, he entered an amazing 284 five-mile races, winning every one of them.

Soon afterward, he successfully raced all over Europe, finally returning home to a full life of roller skating, giving exhibitions and managing rinks until his death in 1950.

Flora and Fauna

In America's agricultural regions, skating rink entrepreneurs sometimes based their roller rink's image, as well as its promotion, upon the local produce. The result often was an eye-catching sticker, as demonstrated by the couple below as they merrily skate their way across a "Greeley Spud." Animals, on the other hand, might have helped sell a rink's wholesome family character—although Morey's mosquito mascot on page 90 was a tip-off that customers should arrive with a sense of humor and perhaps some insect repellent.

NORTH ST. MARYS · SAN ANTONIO
TWINKLE TWIRPS

THE NATIONAL
SKATING CLUB
"THE ARENA TABBIES"
MIDDLETOWN, R.I.

TONY
THE
WONDER
CHIMP

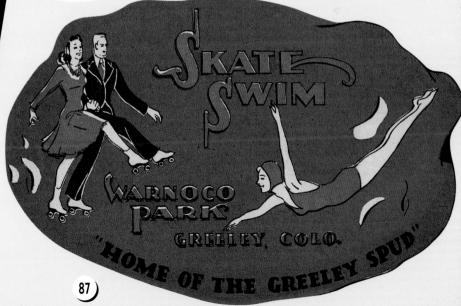

SKATE SWIM
WARNOCO PARK
GREELEY, COLO.
"HOME OF THE GREELEY SPUD"

WATERTOWN
SPIDER'S
ROLLER SKATING
STONY WEB POINT
SOUTH DAKOTA

BLOOMINGTON ILLINOIS
ROLLER
CIRCUS RINK

WONDERLAND ROLLER RINK
5425 EASTON AVE.
ST. LOUIS, MO.

ONLY CONTENTED SKATERS SKATE AT
BEATY'S ROLLERENA
SIX MILES SOUTH
OF
HUNTINGTON
IND
9 & 37

ROLLARENA
Peanut Rollers
RICHMOND

LAKEPARK
4 MI.
NORTH
CORVALLIS
ROLLER RINK

Roller Skating Rink

VENICE, FLORIDA

Cardinal

IOWA'S FINEST

IIDTOWN ROLLER RINK

DES MOINES, IOWA.

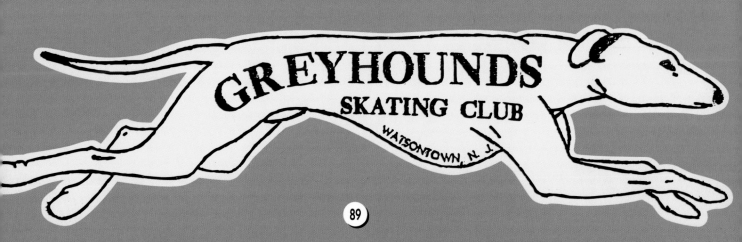

GREYHOUNDS
SKATING CLUB
WATSONTOWN, N. J.

BAL-A-ROUE MEDFORD, MASS.

BAL-A-ROUE MEDFORD, MASS.

TO BAL-A-ROUE MEDFORD

CLEAN HEALTHFUL FUN

Fox ROLLER RINK

ELGIN, ILLINOIS

...NG THE YEAR ROUND

Morey's RIVERVIEW Roller Rink Pennsville N.J.

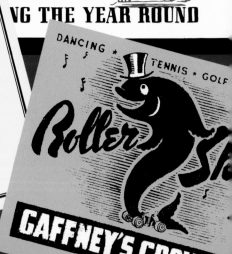

DANCING ♪ TENNIS ★ GOLF

Roller

GAFFNEY'S GROVE at WIL...

GREAT
LEOPARD

ROLLER SKATING RINK
CHESTER, PA.

ROLLER-PALACE
ROCHESTER, N.Y.

JAYHAWK
KANSAS
CITY
KANSAS
RINK

ROLLER at SKATE
WILDWOOD
Steep Falls, Maine

ELI SKATING CLUB · NEW HAVEN, CONN.

CRYSTAL PALACE
ROLLER   SKATING
CRYSTAL
3301 GERMANTOWN AVE.

PENGUIN CLUB
WINNWOOD RINK

BERRYVILLE
BERRYVILLE
VA.
ROLLER RINK

BONDA
SKATELAND
-ROUTE 22-
PAWLING, N.Y.

Skate your Date at HIGHLAND LAKE PAVILION RINK WINSTED, CONN.

COLISEUM SKATING RINK
MEMBER R.S.R.O.A.
DAVIS ISLANDS TAMPA ☆ FLORIDA

EAST PROVIDENCE ROLLER RINK
Member of R.S.R.O.A.

Woolleys ROLLER RINK
460 SOUTH STATE
WOOLLY RINK
SALT LAKE CITY, UTAH

TURKS ROLLERDROME
PRIVATE PARTIES PHONE
PEN ARGYL 330 J
BANGOR PEN ARGYL HIGHWAY · PENNA ·

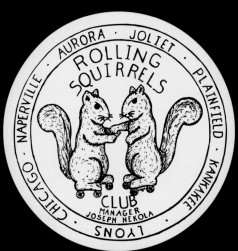

AURORA · JOLIET
NAPERVILLE · ROLLING SQUIRRELS · PLAINFIELD
CHICAGO · KANKAKEE
LYONS
CLUB
MANAGER JOSEPH NEKOLA

FOX VALLEY ROLLER RINK
NEENAH
WIS.

GROUNDHOG ROLLER RINK
PUNXSUTAWNEY, PA.

BOB-O-LINK SKATE CLUB
POST LAKE
ELCHO, WIS.

MAMMOTH GARDEN

ROLLER SKATING

• RINK •

1540 CLARKSON-DENVER,COLO.

Wings on Wheels

GREEN-TOP ROLLER RINK JOPLIN M.O.

The very first person who had the courage to whiz along on roller skates probably blurted out two things: "It's as if there are *wings* on my feet!" and "Somebody help me—I can't stop!" Wings on our feet have connoted the image of speed in our minds ever since Mercury was given the job of mes-

Kids from Detroit proudly show off their Arena Gardens Roller Skating Club patches and stickers after some organized fun in 1938.

MAPLE GROVE ROLLARENA

MAPLE GROVE PARK

LANCASTER, PA.

ARENA GARDENS ROLLER SKATING CLUB of DETROIT

TUCSON ROLLER RINK in the SUNSHINE CITY OF ARIZONA

SEFFERINO ROLLERDROME CINCINNATI

Facing page: The winged skating signage in this 1955 postcard detail seems almost to be a UFO that's decided that the roof of Skateland in Phoenix, Arizona, is as good a landing site as any.

senger to the ancient gods. Nothing will keep you moving faster than Zeus when he wants something in a hurry!

Throughout the Golden Age, skating sticker graphics varied greatly. While some rinks featured illuminated signs urging skaters to slow down and enjoy the slow graceful glide of a waltz-time organ tempo, the speedy icon of the winged roller skate still seemed ever so prevalent. And let's face it, when it comes time to take to that maple floor, it requires a lot of willpower to keep the speed down!

GAYWAY ROLLER RINK NEOSHO, MO.

S. AND M. ROLLER RINK
1840 West 33rd So
Salt Lake City

LINCOLN PARK Roller Skating Rink
2037 LINCOLN PARK AVENUE LOS ANGELES
AVAILABLE FOR PRIVATE PARTIES

TREE CITY ROLLER DROME · GREENSBURG, IND.

KEARNY *Roller* SKATING RINK
1100 HARRISON AVE. KEARNY, NEW JERSEY

Taking us back to the days when much roadside advertising was wonderfully home-made, this giant plywood replica of a winged skate looms out of the trees in Salem, Oregon—a convincing enticement to stop in and roller skate anytime!

Celina Ohio
EDGEWATER ROLLER RINK

ACE ROLLER RINK HIGH
· JANESVILLE, WIS. ·

MOOSIC ROLLER RINK
· MOOSIC ROAD ·
OLD FORGE, PA.

ARENA ROLLER RINK
ST. LOUIS

SANTA ROSA
SANTA ROSA ROLLER RINK

FAIRFIELD ROLLER RINK
LANCASTER OHIO

ALTON BAY N.H.
PAVILION

ROLLARENA

DOWNERS GROVE
ILLINOIS

CARROLL,
IOWA

20th CENTURY
ROLLER RINK

HEALDSBURG
CALIF.

RIVER GARDEN
ROLLERDROME

PLACERVILLE
CALIF.

MOTOR CITY
RINK

LAROSE GARDEN
RINK
LEHIGHTON, PA.

CANTON,
O.

LAND·O·DANCE
ROLLER RINK

NEW LEXINGTON
OHIO

FIORE'S
ROLLER SKATING
RINK
PERRY COUNTY

SKATELAND
FT. SMITH, ARK.

BUFFALO
N.Y.

MAIN
RINK

OAK LAWN
ILLINOIS
ROLLER RINK
9121 SO. CICERO AVE.

RIVERSIDE ROLLERDROME
THE FRIENDLY RINK
Jacksonville, Fla.

WILLOW LAKE
SCHUYLKILL
HAVEN, PA
Swimming
Roller
Skating

PACIFIC
SKATING RINK
San Diego's
Largest and Finest
FRONT & "G" STS.
San Diego
4 5

WM. T. BROWN
SOUTHGATE
FIGURE SKATING CLUB
R-S-R-O-A

WHIRL-A-WAY
BROOKVILLE OHIO

PARADISE
NO. 2
ROLLER RINK
ST. MARYS OHIO

The HUB

YEAR AROUND
ROLLER SKATING

GIANT
ROLLER RINK

4510 N. HARLEM · CHICAGO 31, ILL.
FREE PARKING

The *Rinks*

ROLLER SKATING
Come on let's go

Even as the roller skating rink industry struggled to bounce back from decline following its Victorian Era boom years, many optimistic owners persevered in building more rinks as early as the 1920s. By mid-century, there were more than 2,100 roller skating rinks across America—from the rurally modest to the metropolitanly spectacular.

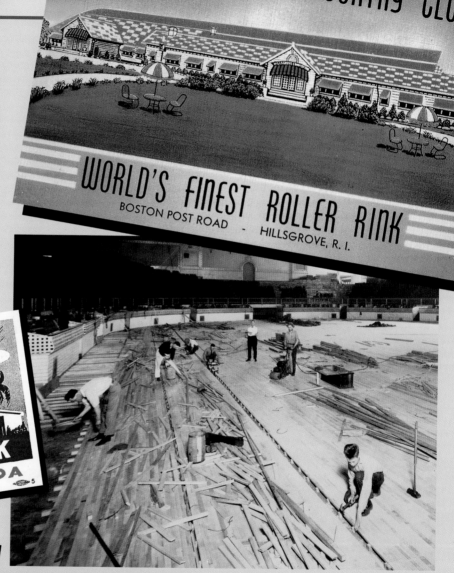

SHOLES HILLSGROVE COUNTRY CLUB

WORLD'S FINEST ROLLER RINK
BOSTON POST ROAD - HILLSGROVE, R. I.

RUSTIC ROLLER RINK
RUSTIC ROLLER RINK
HIALEAH, FLORIDA

ROGERS' RINK

"Hello, this is Art."

"Yes, we skate every night except Monday, 7:30 till 10:00."

CAPITOL BEACH
LINCOLN, NEBRASKA

Above: *Craftsmen meticulously piece together the intricacies of a skating rink floor at Kansas City's Convention Hall in 1925.* **Top:** *The beautiful Sholes Hillsgrove Country Club facade elegantly masks the massive roller skating rink behind it. It recently closed its doors for good, after more than 60 years, as one of the oldest rinks in the country.*

SKYLINE ROLLER RINK
Topeka, Kansas

8TH & WALNUT STS.
DES MOINES, IOWA
CAPLE'S MIDTOWN
ROLLER RINK
HAMMOND ORGAN

MID CITY RINK
NY
ALBANY
MENANDS
TROY
WATERVLIET

MANHATTAN
TEN MINUTES FROM TIMES SQUARE
RDROME
LEXINGTON AVE., NEW YORK

uring the 1940s and 1950s, roller skating took New York City by storm with dozens of rinks and major skating events that were featured at places like Madison Square Garden. The *New York Journal-American* ran a column twice a week devoted to nothing but roller skating!

Every American city featured a flagship skating rink of which they were proud, and for New York, it was Gay Blades. Stylishly located at 239 West 52nd Street in the upper region of Times Square, it was considered by many to be the most beautiful rink ever built. The rink's owners also owned its sister building right around the corner that happened to house Roseland—the world's most famous dance hall. Dancing and dining meant bigger profits than skating and hot dogs, so when the dance hall's building was sold in 1956, they moved Roseland into the Gay Blades space. The rink was closed forever, but Roseland still thrives there today—a palatial ghost of what Gay Blades must have been.

For HEALTH'S sake and FUN
Let's Go
ROLLER SKATING
10:30 A.M. EVERY MORNING 50¢
2:30 P.M. EVERY AFTERNOON 50¢
5:30 P.M. EVERY AFTERNOON 50¢
8:30 P.M. EVERY EVENING 65¢
including Skate Rental
MIDNIGHT SESSION 65¢
SATURDAY
GAY BLADES
America's Most Palatial ROLLER Skating Rink
52nd ST. West of B'WAY ★ Circle 7-4177
Popular Priced

PLAYLAND

LINCOLN HIGHWAY—3 MILES EAST OF YORK, PENNA.

GUPTILL ARENA

36,000 SQUARE FEET TO SKATE UPON

RT. 9, BOGHT CORNERS
CE. 7-6223

ALBANY-SARATOGA RD.
2 MI. NORTH OF LATHAM CIRCLE

"THE BRIGHTEST SPOT ON THE GREAT LAKES"

BIG PAVILION
SAUGATUCK
MICHIGAN

PALISADE GARDENS

TELEPHONE
W. 5085
·
No. 7 BUS
TO OUR DOOR

ROLLER
SKATING
Every
NIGHT

2938 UNIVERSITY AVE.
SAN DIEGO, CALIF.

UTAH

THE FINEST ON THE LAKE SHORE
ARDON
ROLLER SKATING
RINK
HWY 42 ½ MI. NORTH OF ZION ILL.

SHOLES

RIVERVIEW
DANCING

SHOLES

RIVERVIEW
ROLLER SKATING

GALLIVAN BLVD.
AT NEPONSET CIRCLE
DORCHESTER, MASS.

SKATING ★ DANCING

CURVECREST
MUSKEGON MICHIGAN

BELVEDERE ROLLER RINK
WEST PALM BEACH, FLORIDA

Skate with Me!

BELVEDERE ROLLER RINK

hollywood ROLLERBOWL
WARNER BROS SUNSET BLVD STUDIOS
WORLDS GREATEST SKATING RINK

TE YOUR DATE WIT
E STARS

KENNEDY ROLLER RINK
"If You Can Walk... You Can Skate"
KENNEDY ROLLER RINK
NOKOMIS ILL.

As the Golden Age unfolded, rinks of
all types abounded. New York had its
Gay Blades, and Hollywood had its
Rollerbowl—promoted as "The World's
Greatest Roller Skating Rink"—where
you could find yourself roller skating
with movie stars at any given moment.
In the background, a postcard features
Charles "Shay" Bedient, the Rollerbowl's proud, well-dressed manager, as
he poses in front of the rink's glamorous interior.

113

114

SCOTCH PINE ROLLER RINK

LAKE DELTON WISCONSIN

SANDWICH ROLLER RINK

SANDWICH ILLINOIS

COLISEUM

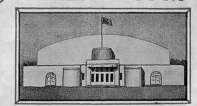

Roller Rink

LORAIN OHIO

ROLLER DOME SKATING RINK

FT. WAYNE, IND.

MELODY SKATELAND

RICHMOND INDIANA

JOYLAND ROLLER RINK
BEARDSTOWN ILL.

The simplicity of open air tent rinks contrasts greatly with the glamorous neon sophistication of Skateland in San Diego, California. Most portable tent rink operators did business far from the big cities and felt that traveling from town to town ensured playing to a freshly packed rink in each new town it visited.

SANDY's ROLLER RINK
JERSEYVILLE, ILL.

POP'S
OPEN AIR ROLLER RINK
THREE RIVERS

San Diego's LARGEST and FINEST

SKATELAND

FRONT and G STS.
Downtown
San Diego
Calif.

SKATING

land

ER SKATING

Skateland

Skateland

SKATING

ROLLER SKATING

FRONT
&
'G' STREETS,
SAN DIEGO 1,
CALIF.

U. S. Grant Hotel

BROADWAY

G. STREET   MARKET

Skateland

Heavens Above

STARLITE
BI-CITY ARENA
FISHERSVILLE, VA.

STARLAND
HAGERSTOWN
MD.

To most roller skaters, "skating under the stars" usually meant skating under the romantic spell of that staple of so many roller rinks—the mirror ball. First introduced as a lighting effect in the Art Deco ballrooms of the '20s and '30s, it was soon causing "oohs" and "ahhs" at roller rinks from coast to coast. With the rink lighting lowered to almost total darkness, skaters would suddenly find themselves skating among thousands of swirling stars and planets. The effect was actually achieved by the simplest of devices—a large ball in the ceiling covered with hundreds of mirror fragments that reflected the colored beams from spotlights as it was slowly turned by an electric motor. Simple—but to skating couples holding hands under its spell, it was like flying among the heavens above.

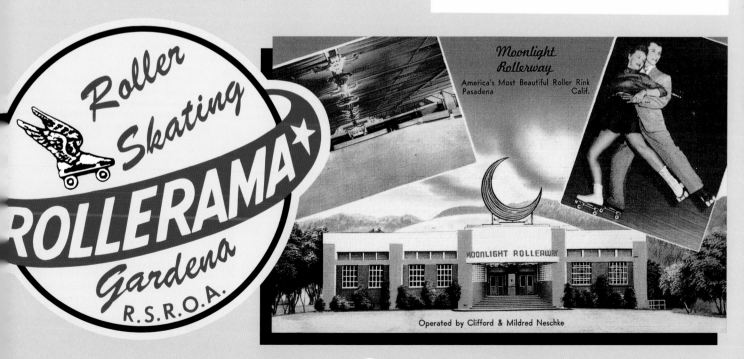

Roller Skating
ROLLERAMA
Gardena
R.S.R.O.A.

Moonlight Rollerway
America's Most Beautiful Roller Rink
Pasadena   Calif.

MOONLIGHT ROLLERWAY

Operated by Clifford & Mildred Neschke

MOONLIGHT · SKATING · PALACE
R·S·R·O·A
YEAR ROUND SKATING
HAMMOND ORGAN
BRADLEY, ILL.

The NEW MOON
ROLLER RINK
ROLLER SKATE FOR HEALTHS' SAKE
CARLISLE, PA.

SILVER MOON ROLLER RINK
1 MILE SO. OF WATERLOO, IND.

FLEETWOOD
ROLLER · RINK
7231 WEST ARCHER AVENUE
SUMMIT, ILLINOIS

N. ST. MARYS ROLLER RINK
Home of STARLIGHTERS CLUB
SAN ANTONIO TEX.
1616 N. ST. MARYS ST.

120

OLYMPIC PARK RINK IRVINGTON N.J.

CUT US OUT

SILVER STAR ROLLER RINK
KALAMAZOO MICHIGAN

M. C. DANBURY, CONN. ROLLER RINK

GOLDEN STAR ROLLER RINK MANLEY, IA.

-STAR SKATING RINK- -S- JACKSON, MISSISSIPPI

SILVER STAR ROLLER RINK
MATTOON, ILL.
J.W. SHIELDS

STAR ROLL ARENA
Missouri's Most Modern Roller Rink   2122 S. Glenstone, Springfield

MY HOME RINK IS ROLLER STARLIGHT SKATING COMPTON

VAN CORTLANDT ROLLER RINK
BROADWAY AT 241ST ST. NYC

Faraway Places

The passion for roller skating was not only limited to the United States. Places as nearby as Mexico and Canada, or as far away as South Africa, all caught a healthy dose of roller rink fever. In Hawaii and the Philippines, American occupation during the War brought with it American culture, including bowling, as shown in the stippled sticker to the right.

A WORLD OF FUN

MANILA ROLLER SKATING RINK, INC.
ROLLER CITY
★★★ MANILA, PHILIPPINES ★★★

TIA JUANA · MEXICO

Visit MAIN STREET RINK
JOHANNESBURG
SOUTH AFRICA

ALOHA
Rainbow
ROLLERLAND
HONOLULU, HAWAII
G.R.O.A.

SKATING
Skate With Me!
PHONE: RUS. 2655.
BUS 40 OR BUS 53
BIRCH PARK
MANCHESTER ENGLAND
SKATING PALACE

SKATELAND
CANADA'S EVERGREEN PLAYGROUND
BRITISH COLUMBIA
NEW WESTMINSTER

Capilano
ROLLERCADE
North Vancouver, B.C.

BRITISH COLUMBIA
CANADA
NATIONAL ROLLER GARDEN
756 YATES STREET
VICTORIA, B.C.

CIVIC AUDITORIUM ROLLER SKATING RINK
ALOHA
MAPLE FLOOR
FIBRE SKATES
HAWAII
HONOLULU, T. H.

HALL'S ROLLER RINK

MT. VERNON ILL.

EGYPT'S FINEST

Miscellany

This last chapter could be called the book's attic. It's piled with stuff that there just wasn't room for elsewhere—mostly items that simply refuse to fit into any existing category, but are just too fascinating to be excluded. It is here that you'll find cards accusing you of stealing and cussin', roller skating alarm clocks, winged jack-o-lanterns, and Egyptian sphinxes in the middle of Illinois.

SKATELAND ARENA BATTLE CREEK MICH

LAKEVIEW
VASA PARK
HAMMOND ORGAN
?
WHITE FLOOR
LAKE SAMMAMISH
SKATING RINK

ULTRA-MODERN ROLLERLAND
926 N. PENN — INDIANAPOLIS
WORLD'S FINEST ROLLER SKATING FLOOR

Some rinks felt a little good-natured humor softened the blow of crowd discipline. The humor often leaned toward a more lowbrow "har-dee-har-har" school of fun, as evidenced by the cards below that were slipped to offending skaters.

LIKE L IT'S YOURS
ROLLER PALACE SKATING ROCHESTER, N. Y.
PUT IT BACK !

GLIDERS SKATING CLUB
LOWE BIRMINGHAM

LIKE HELL IT'S YOURS
PUT IT BACK
KAHLER
YORKTOWN INDIANA

Instructions
(inside)
for those
who want to
"CUSS"

SHUT UP!

With the compliments of
THE ARENA RECREATION CENTER
Washington, Pa.

GAY-WAY
ROLLER RINK & PO
R.D. #2 HARRISBURG
SKATE-SWIM
SWIM IN WAT FIT TO DRINK
MIDNITE SKATING EVERY SAT. NITE
PICNICS AMUSEMENTS
"TOPS THEM ALL FOR FUN"

ETA HUNKA
CAMDEN, N. J.

NORWOOD Rink
GREATER G[...]

PARAMOUNT SKATING RINK
WAVERLY BEACH
BELOIT WISCONSIN
NO 2

GREEN'S PLA-MOR RINK
C
CONNERSVILLE IND.

WHIRLING WHEELS
MONROE, WIS.
ROLLER [...]

ROLLERLAND
AKRON
OHIO

SKATE WITH "SPEC" SAUNDERS
123 EL-PASEO
REDONDO BEACH CALIF.
REDON[...] [...]TELAND
R.S.R.O.A.

SPOTLITE ROLLER RINK
66
LA GRANGE ILL.

HILLSIDE
— ROLLER RINK —
LAKE PARK

131

NEW HAMPSHIRE'S LARGEST AND FINEST RINK
Arcadia Skating Rink
MASSABESIC LAKE   MANCHESTER, N.H.

EXTON
ROLLER RINK

OF THE WEST WHITELAND FIRE CO.

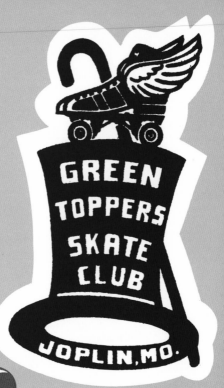

GREEN
TOPPERS
SKATE
CLUB

JOPLIN, MO.

FAIRFIELD ROLLER RINK
LANCASTER, OHIO
ONE OF THE
"BETTER RINKS"

DERBY ROLLER RINK
Derby, Colo.

P.C. Petersen, Prop.

LOG CABIN ROLLER RINK

NORTH LAKE ST. ROAD   P. O.
NO. AURORA, ILLIN...

OLD MILL SKATING RINK
GLOUCESTER VA.
ORGAN MUSIC
IT IS FUN TO SKATE AT THE OLD MILL

Greetings from

THRESA
PHYLLIS   PATSY
MARTIN   CAROL
JUNIOR   MARILYN
MA   PA

ARTISTIC ROLLER RINK

CASTLE · BARN

ST. RD. 3...
S ¼...
MARTINSVILLE IND.

ROLLER RINK

FOR · AN · EVENING
⊞ OF ⊞ FUN ⊞
ON WHEELS

As the popularity of roller skating spread to the hinterland, both permanent and traveling rinks dotted the rural American landscape in all sizes and styles. Butch Laufer (affectionately known as "Pa" to his customers) managed the Artistic Roller Rink with the help of his family near West Bend, Wisconsin.

MERRY CHRISTMAS

AND A

HAPPY NEW YEAR

oops! It's a

BROUGHT UP TO DATE

M.J.Sanders

Happy New Year!

Merry Christmas and

BE A "GOOD SKATE"

VALENTINE!

ROLLER JACK O LANTERN CLUB

HOLIDAY GREETINGS

To My

A Birthday Note

There was so much camaraderie among skating enthusiasts that skate-related correspondence abounded throughout the year. All of the cards shown here—except the jack-o-lantern and the valentine shown lower left— were created by Margaret J. Sanders, whom some called the "Grandma Moses" of skating art (see page 23).

WEBSTER SQ. ARENA

Skate for health and pleasure

WORCESTER 3 ....MASS....

JOHN'S RINK

STATE 33 U.S. 45 U.S. 40
U.S. 40 STATE 33
U.S. 45 60'X150'
HEART OF U.S.A.

...NGHAM, ILLINO...

BEBE'S SKATING

Bowling — Carpet Golf

MARIANNA, FLORIDA

CASINO ROLLER

Skate for hea... a... pleas...

VALLEJO CALIFORN...

DALAMAR ROLLER RINK
THE HEART OF MONTGOMERY CO.
Gaithersburg, Md.

SEA SKATING

New ...ple Floor

SALISBURY BEACH

Oce...

MASS.

138

Bibliography

Curtis, Susan. "Mineola Skating Rink, the Home of Dance Skating." *Historical Roller Skating Overview.* October/November, 1998.

Fried, Chester. "Rink Stickers—It's History." *The Roller Skaters' Gazette.* March, 1999.

Fried, Chester. "Rolling Along: The History of the Skate Queen." *Rinksider.* January/February, 2003.

Love, Bill. "Sticker Collecting." *Roller Skating Annual.* 1948-1949.

"The Lowe Family Operation." *Historical Roller Skating Overview.* February/March, 1997.

"The RSROA Celebrates 60!" *Historical Roller Skating Overview.* April/May, 1997.

Svec, Frank. "Start That Trading Today!" *The International Roller Skating Guide.* 1949-1950 Edition.

"Troops May Move on Roller Skates to Save Gasoline and Tire Rubber." *Popular Science.* November, 1942.

Turner, James. *History of Roller Skating.* Lincoln, Nebraska: Roller Skating Rink Operators Association of America, 1975.

Turner, James with Michael Zaidman. *The History of Roller Skating.* Lincoln, Nebraska: The National Museum of Roller Skating, 1997.

Wallis, Deborah L. "Her Royal Highness, Our Skate Queen." *Historical Roller Skating Overview.* January, 2002.

Webber, Sarah. *The Allure of the Rink: Roller Skating at the Arena Gardens.* Lincoln, Nebraska: The National Museum of Roller Skating, 1999.

Webber, Sarah. "The Bug That Bites: Roller Rink Sticker Collecting." *Historical Roller Skating Overview.* July, 2002.

Webber, Sarah. "Follies on Wheels: The Skating Vanities, 1940-1955." *Historical Roller Skating Overview.* February/March, 1998.

Webber, Sarah. "1900-1997: A Century of Rinking Across the United States." *Historical Roller Skating Overview.* April/May, 1998.

Wilhite, Scott A. *The Evolution of the Roller Skate: 1820–Present.* Lincoln, Nebraska: The National Museum of Roller Skating, 1994.

Picture Credits

The National Museum of Roller Skating: photographs on pp. 2-3, 8, 10, 12, 13-17, 19, 36, 38, 43, 58, 63, 70-71, 76-77, 82-83, 85, 95, 107, 108-109; "Both Ways" card, 12; Sheet Music, 72; "Tony the Wonder Chimp" postcard, 87; "Skateland" postcard, 97 • **Chicago Roller Skate Co.:** roller skates, 7; comic book excerpt from "Skating Skills—Secrets of Skating" © 1957, 44; postcard, 45; postcard, 46; "Popular as Your Best Date" advertisement, 51 • Stickers and greeting cards created by Margaret J. Sanders are used by permission of Chester Fried • Images of Gloria Nord from 1946 and 1948 Skating Vanities • All other images in *Skate Crazy* are from the collection of the author.

Every reasonable effort has been made by the author to obtain the rights to images displayed in *Skate Crazy.* If you feel any acknowledgments have been overlooked, please contact the publisher, and the information will be considered for subsequent editions.

The Rink Index

ALABAMA
Bessemer
Monterey Roller Rink, 135
Birmingham
Lowe's Gliders Club, 61, 130
Rambling Rollers, 134
Phenix City
Idle Hour Park Roller Rink, 55

ARIZONA
Douglas
Johnson's Skateland, 70
Phoenix
Rollerdrome, 83
Skateland, 97
Tucson
Pastime Park Roller Rink, 81
Sunset Rollerama, 84
Tucson Roller Rink, 96

ARKANSAS
Fort Smith
Skateland, 103
Jonesboro
Community Roller Drome, 71
Little Rock
D & C Roller Rink, 51, 134

CALIFORNIA
Anaheim
Valencia Skating Rink, 86
Escondido
Ups-N-Downs Roller Rink, 53
Fairfax
Cocoanut Grove Skating Rink, 78
Fairfield
Redman's Roller Rink, 45
Gardena
Rollerama, 119
Healdsburg
River Garden Rollerdrome, 64, 103
Long Beach
Hippodrome Skating Rink, 33
Los Angeles
Hollywood Rollerbowl, 21, 45, 113
Lincoln Park Roller Skating Rink, 97
Redondo Skateland, 131
Shrine Roller Rink, 98
Starlight Roller Skating, 123
Oakland
Skatemor Rink, 55
Pacific Grove
Skateland, 72
Pasadena
Moonlight Rollerway, 119
Paso Robles
Paso Robles Roller Rink, 57
Placerville
Motor City Rink, 103
Pomona
Pastime Roller Rink, 100
Salinas
Salinas Rollerland, 81

San Diego
Pacific Skating Rink, 104
Palisade Gardens, 112
Skateland, 117
San Rafael
Marin Skateland, 69
Santa Ana
Santa Ana Roller Rink, 33
Skate Ranch, 85
Santa Barbara
Rollercade Skating Rink, 74
Santa Rosa
Santa Rosa Roller Rink, 77, 102
29 Palms
29 Palms Rollerink, 83
Vallejo
Casino Roller Rink, 64, 138

COLORADO
Colorado Springs
Pikes Peak Skateland, 83
Denver
Mammoth Garden Rink, 94
Skateland, 30
Derby
Derby Roller Rink, 132
Greeley
Warnoc Park, 87
Manitou Springs
Manitou Roller Rink, 83

CONNECTICUT
Bantam Lake
Music Box Roller Rink, 72
Bridgeport
Holland's Skateland, 30
Park City Skateland, 78
Danbury
Y.M.C.C. Roller Rink, 122
Groton
Melody Skating Rink, 75
New Britain
Doyle's Skating Rink, 65
New Haven
Eli Skating Club, 92
Norwalk
Kid Beans Roller Rink, 98
Winsted
Highland Lake Pavilion Rink, 93

FLORIDA
Cayo Hueso
Tommie's, 100
Hialeah
Rustic Roller Rink, 107
Jacksonville
Riverside Rollerdrome, 104
Marianna
Bebe's Skating, 138
Sanford
Melodee Roller Rink, 50

Sulphur Springs
Palace Skating Rink, 64
Tampa
Coliseum Skating Rink, 93
Venice
Cardinal Roller Skating Rink, 89
West Palm Beach
Belvedere Roller Rink, 113

GEORGIA
Atlanta
Rollerdrome, 54, 56
Columbus
Rhythm Rollers, 76

HAWAII
Honolulu
Civic Auditorium, 126
Rainbow Rollerland, 125

IDAHO
Boise
Boise Roller Club, 134

ILLINOIS
Alton
Playmor Skating Arena, 134
Arlington Heights
Arlington Roller Rink, 82
Aurora/North Aurora
Log Cabin Roller Rink, 133
Parkview Roller Rink, 45
Beardstown
Joyland Roller Rink, 116
Belvidere
Fox Skating Palace, 98
Bloomington
Circus Roller Rink, 88
Bradley
Moonlight Skating Palace, 120
Chicago
Armory Roller Skating Club, 51
The Hub Giant Roller Rink, 106
New Planet Roller Rink, 118
Rolling Squirrels Club, 93
Swank Rink, 39
Dallas City
Italian Village, 67
Danville
Proud's Recreation, 98
Decatur
Regal Roller Rink, 37
Downers Grove
Rollarena, 103
Effingham
John's Rink, 138
Elgin
Fox Roller Rink, 90
Jerseyville
Sandy's Roller Rink, 116
Kankakee
Palace Roller Rink, 38
La Grange
Spotlight 66 Roller Rink, 131

Markham
Melody Bowl Roller Rink, 32
Mattoon
Silver Star Roller Rink, 123
Mt. Vernon
Hall's Roller Rink, 128
Nokomis
Kennedy Roller Rink, 113
Oak Lawn
Oak Lawn Roller Rink, 104
Pekin
Blue Island Roller Rink, 135
Peoria
Fernwood Rink, 98
Rockford
Paramount Roller Rink, 68
Sandwich
Fairway Skating Palace, 74
Sandwich Roller Rink, 115
Springfield
Moonlight Garden Skating Palace, 62
Summit
Fleetwood Roller Rink, 120
Zion
Ardon Roller Skating Rink, 112

INDIANA
Anderson
Anderson Roller Rink, 85
Connersville
Green's Pla-Mor Rink, 131
Decatur
Happy Hours Roller Rink, 129
Fort Wayne
Roller Dome Skating Rink, 115
Greensburg
Tree City Roller Drome, 101
Hammond
Palace Roller Rink, 39
Roller Dome, 41
State Skating Rink, 29
Huntington
Beaty's Rollerena, 88
Indianapolis
Rollerland, 130
True Blue Roller Club, 18
Lafayette
Aca y Alla Roller Rink, 84
Marion
Idyl Wyld Roller Rink, 110
Martinsville
Castle Barn Roller Rink, 133
Richmond
Melody Skateland, 115
Russiaville
Rol A Way Skating Rink, 61
Yorktown
Kahler Roller Rink, 130

IOWA

Ames
Skateland, 83
Carroll
20th Century Roller Rink, 103
Cedar Falls
Black Hawk Roller Rink, 83
Clinton
Petersen Roller Rink, 100
Denison
Stardom Roller Rink, 98
Des Moines
Midtown Roller Rink, 89, 109
Indianola
Roundup Rink, 84
Manley
Golden Star Roller Rink, 122

KANSAS

Kansas City
Jayhawk Rink, 91
Topeka
Rol-A-Way Roller Rink, 98
Skyline Roller Rink, 109
Wichita
Alaskan, 67
Melody Rink, 75

KENTUCKY

Louisville
Cholley's Rollatorium, 20

LOUISIANA

Monroe
Gus Kallio Roller Rink, 139
Shreveport
Ludendi Roller Drome, 114

MAINE

Steep Falls
Wildwood, 91

MARYLAND

Baltimore
Carlin's Park, 19
Gaithersburg
Dalamar Roller Rink, 138
Hagerstown
Starland, 119

MASSACHUSETTS

Cambridge
Tech Rollerway, 38
Dorchester
Sholes Riverview, 112
Medford
Bal-A-Roue, 90
Mendon
Nipmuc Park Roller Rink, 80
Pittsfield
Crystal Palace Skating Rink, 34
Salibury Beach
Sea View Skating Rink, 138
Webster
Indian Rollers, 81
Worcester
Webster Sq. Arena, 138

MICHIGAN

Battle Creek
Skateland Arena, 130
Detroit
Arena Gardens, 71, 95
Grand Rapids
Ramona Gardens, 73
Irons
Loon Lake Pavilion, 39
Kalamazoo
Silver Star Roller Rink, 122
Muskegon
Curvecrest, 113
New Buffalo
Scotty's Roller Bowl, 45
Saugatuck
Big Pavilion, 112
Southgate
Wm. T. Brown Figure Skating Club, 105
Sturgis
Pop's Open Air Roller Rink, 13
Three Rivers
Pop's Open Air Roller Rink, 116

MINNESOTA

Albert Lea/New Ulm
Carl's Roller Rinks, 42
Cokato
Cokato Rollerdrome, 134
Hutchinson
Ted's Roller Rink, 73
Mankato
Imperial Rink, 58
Minneapolis
Cub's Rollerdrome, 135
St. Louis Park
Pastime Arena, 77

MISSISSIPPI

Jackson
Star Skating Rink, 122

MISSOURI

Hannibal
Rol-Arena, 134
Joplin
Green-Top Roller Rink, 95
Green Toppers Skate Club, 132
Kansas City
Heart of America Roller Rink, 34
Neosho
Gayway Roller Rink, 97
Springfield
Star Roll Arena, 123
St. Louis
Arena Roller Rink, 102
Wonderland Roller Rink, 88
Winnwood
Winnwood Rink, 92

NEBRASKA

Beatrice
Van's Roller Rink, 49
Lincoln
Rogers' Rink, 107

Omaha
Crosstown Roller Rink, 38

NEVADA

Elko
Silver State Roller Rink, 135

NEW HAMPSHIRE

Alton Bay
Pavilion, 102
Manchester
Arcadia Skating Rink, 132
Nashua
Turnpike Rollaway, 135
Rochester
Humoresque, 32

NEW JERSEY

Belleville
Riviera Park Roller Rink, 70
Bridgeton
Radio Barn, 85
Camden
Eta Hunka Pi, 130
Florham Park
Florham Park Arena, 55
Irvington
Olympic Park Rink, 121
Kearny
Kearny Roller Skating Rink, 101
Mays Landing
Lake Lenape Rink, 29
Neptune
Shore Roller Drome, 79
Pennsville
Morey's Riverview Roller Rink, 90
Red Bank
Singing Wheels Arena, 74
South Amboy
South Amboy Arena, 69
Trenton
Central Roller Rink, 44
Watsontown
Greyhounds Skating Club, 89
White Horse Roller Rink, 50

NEW MEXICO

Albuquerque
East End Roller Rink, 81

NEW YORK

Albany
Hoffman's Skateland, 55
Midcity Rink, 109
Auburn
Reva Rollerdrome, 111
Boght Corners
Guptill Arena, 111
Buffalo
Main Rink, 103
Scott's Rink, 30
Charlotte
Tom Gierson Rink, 76

Dunkirk
Roll Arena, 53
Endicott
Enjoie Park, 63
Long Island
Mineola Skating Rink, 49
Newburgh
Avalon Roller Drome, 49
New York City
Brooklyn Roller Skating Rink, 63
Coney Island Roller Skating Rink, 4
Eastern Parkway Roller Rink, 32
Gay Blades, 22, 47, 68, 109
Hillside Skating Rink, 67, 68
Manhattan Rollerdrome, 108
Queens Roller Rink, 37
Van Cortlandt Roller Rink, 123
Orangeburg
Orangeburg Playland, 37
Pawling
Bonda Skateland, 92
Rochester
Eddie's Roller Palace, 43
Roller Palace, 91, 130

OHIO

Akron
Rollerland, 131
Brookville
Whirl-A-Way, 105
Canton
Land-O-Dance Roller Rink, 103
Celina
Edgewater Roller Rink, 29, 101
Cincinnati
Norwood Rink, 131
Sefferino Rollerdrome, 96
Cleveland
Roller Bowl, 98
Columbus
Rollerland, 60
Dayton
Rollerdrome, 64
Genoa
Forest Park Roller Rink, 51
Indian Lake
Orchard Island Skating Rink, 29
Lancaster
Fairfield Roller Rink, 102, 132
Lorain
Coliseum Roller Rink, 115
Rhythm Rollers, 72
New Lexington
Fiore's Roller Skating Rink, 103
St. Marys
Paradise No. 2 Roller Rink, 105
Tiffin
Skateland Roller Rink, 50
Toledo
Kish's Rink, 53

Myers Bros.

ROLLER RINK

IN THE ATOMIC CITY
OF OAK RIDGE, TENN.
BOOM

The End